Disney
HIGH SCHOOL MUSICAL
EAST HIGH MEMORIES

By Emma Harrison

Based on the hit Disney Channel Original Movie
"High School Musical", written by Peter Barsocchini

PaRragon

Bath · New York · Singapore · Hong Kong · Cologne · Delhi · Melbourne

First published by Parragon in 2007
Parragon
Queen Street House
4 Queen Street
Bath BA1 1HE, UK

ISBN 978-1-4075-1106-1

Printed in China

Welcome to East High School!

Hey there, Wildcats!

It's been one crazy year here at East High. Mobile phones were confiscated; chilli fries flew; there was a blackout during the championship basketball game; and one loner transfer student turned the entire social structure of our school on its head. From the sound of it, this year could have been a disaster, right? Wrong! Lots of things changed, but they definitely changed for the better. And this book is chock-full of fabulous memories to help you recall all your favourite moments. We hope you enjoy it!

Sincerely,
The East High School Yearbook Staff

GO WILDCATS!

THE YEAR BEGINS. . . .

This year at East High started out like any other. Old friends welcomed each other back and at least one *new* student was met with open arms as well. The Drama Club, Wildcat basketball team, and Scholastic Decathlon team were all abuzz with activity. Sounds like a lot of excitement, huh? Well there's always tons going on at East High.

Chad welcomes Troy back from winter break.

Auditions for the Winter Musical are coming up!

Troy and Gabriella meet up in the hallway on her first day at East High.

Ryan and Sharpay make a startling discovery in the library: Gabriella is an Einstein-ette!

Sharpay and Troy talk about the big game.

Taylor and Gabriella attempt to speak "cheerleader."

Taylor and Chad put their heads together in the lab.

Troy has a little trouble paying attention in class.

WORK HARD . . .

Whether it's academics, clubs or sports, we here at East High take our work very seriously - most of the time, anyway. . . .

Gabriella and Taylor discuss Scholastic Decathlon strategies at lunch.

Troy lines up for the shot.

Gabriella helps make costumes for the Winter Musical.

That Kelsi is always working on a new arrangement.

Gabriella congratulates Troy with a hug.

. . . AND HAVE FUN!

Singing, dancing, baking, snooping, scheming, shooting hoops, or just plain hanging out, the students of East High sure know how to blow off some steam!

Zeke offers up some crème brûlée.

Uh-oh! It looks like Sharpay and Ryan are hatching a plan.

Ryan just can't hide his enthusiasm.

Troy and the guys get down at an impromptu pep rally.

Chad and Taylor celebrate after the championship game.

Gabriella and Taylor present . . . basketball physics!

Sharpay is really excited about the Winter Musical auditions.

The basketball team hangs in their second home - the locker room.

Troy checks out the musical auditions from a safe distance.

Ryan does a little snooping in the halls.

CALLBACK CANDID!

One of the biggest events of the year was definitely the callback audition for *Twinkle Towne*. For the first time, everyone in the school came out to support, well, everyone else. Check out some of our favourite moments from that incredible day!

Ms Darbus shows her flair for the dramatic.

Troy tells Chad about Gabriella's big win at the Scholastic Decathlon.

Gabriella and Troy dance it up on the basketball court.

Troy gives Kelsi the game ball.

Ryan and Sharpay are ready for their close-up.

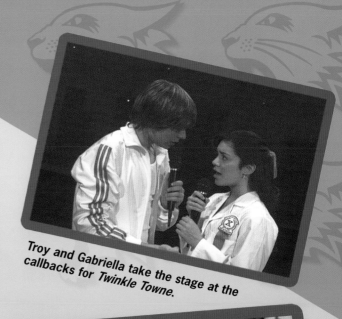

Troy and Gabriella take the stage at the callbacks for *Twinkle Towne.*

Sharpay struts her stuff.

WILD CATS

LET'S PARTY!

Is there a better way to celebrate
a perfect callback, a Scholastic Decathlon win
and the first basketball championship in four years, than
with a huge party in the gym? Ummm . . . we can't think of one!

TROY BOLTON

WILDCATS
14
ATRLETIC DEPT.

Troy was the first-ever second-year student to make the East High varsity basketball team. His teammates unanimously elected him captain, and he went on to lead the squad to a stellar season, bringing them back to the district championship game for the first time in three years. (Go Wildcats!) As the son of Jack Bolton, former East High basketball star and current head coach of the team, we always knew Troy would return the struggling program to glory!

But Troy also surprised everyone, from his classmates to his teachers to his family (and maybe even himself), when he auditioned for the Winter Musical, *Twinkle Towne* . . . and won the male lead! (Hmmm . . . actually, maybe it was Ryan Evans who was more surprised than anyone.) Who knew Troy Bolton, man of many skills on the basketball court, could actually sing? But can he ever! He not only brought down the house during his audition with Gabriella Montez, but who can forget his incredible performance in three straight sold-out shows? Looks like we have a superstar-in-the-making walking the halls of East High. Will Troy be the next LeBron James or the next Justin Timberlake? Maybe both!

All About Troy Bolton

Best Friends: Chad Danforth, Zeke Baylor, Gabriella Montez
Quote: "What team? Wildcats!"
Sports: Varsity Basketball (captain)
Activities: Winter Musical
Never seen without: a friendly smile
Where will you be in ten years?
"Who knows? Hopefully, someplace great.
If there's one thing I've learned this year,
it's that the best things in life are not planned."

Troy and Gabriella hang out in Troy's favourite East High spot, the rooftop garden.

Troy gets soulful during his callback audition with Gabriella.

Troy hoists the championship trophy . . . as his teammates hoist him!

Troy and Chad plan their next move.

GABRIELLA MONTEZ

Gabriella was the new girl in school this year and at first it looked as if she was content to just lay low and blend in. But that changed pretty quickly when Sharpay Evans uncovered Gabriella's secret Einstein-ette past! As it turned out, Gabriella was a major brain and had won all kinds of academic awards at her old school, so of course Taylor McKessie instantly recruited her for the Scholastic Decathlon team. Thanks to Gabriella's sharp pen and even sharper mind, East High crushed our rival, West High, in the biggest academic showdown of the year!

Little did we know that Gabriella wasn't just a bookworm. A member of her church choir for years, Gabriella decided to try out for the Winter Musical and won the female lead. For the first time since anyone at East High could remember, someone other than Sharpay Evans got top billing in a Drama Club production. But although it was cool to see someone new get a shot at stardom, the best part was watching Gabriella come out of her shy shell and shine. (Say that three times fast!) Singing obviously brings this girl all kinds of joy and it was infectious during the three sold-out shows the Drama Club staged this winter. We're glad you came to East High, Gabriella!

All About Gabriella Montez

Best Friends: Taylor McKessie, Troy Bolton, Kelsi Nielsen
Quote: "That should be sixteen over pi."
Activities: Winter Musical, National Honours Society,
Scholastic Decathlon
Never seen without: a book
Where will you be in ten years?
"Doing something I love."

Gabriella can make even the toughest problem understandable.

Gabriella shows off her Wildcat spirit!

Gabriella practises her audition piece with Kelsi.

Troy and Gabriella race to rehearsal.

SHARPAY EVANS

Sharpay is, and always has been, one of those people who knows who she is and is not afraid to flaunt it. Since kindergarten she has been our class's number one fashion plate and dramatic superstar. She has won the starring role in every play and musical East High has staged since she was a first-year student. And she never doubted for a second that she would be the lead in this year's production of *Twinkle Towne*. That's probably why she was so incredibly freaked when she first heard Gabriella Montez's singing voice. It was the first time Sharpay was faced with any real competition.

We all know what happened next. At Sharpay's suggestion, Ms Darbus moved the callback auditions so that they would take place at the same time as Troy's championship basketball game and Gabriella's Scholastic Decathlon match. Then, by some crazy freak accident (wink, wink), both Troy and Gabriella's events were put on hold, and they were able to perform after all. In the end, Gabriella won the lead and Sharpay was forced to take a supporting role in *Twinkle Towne*. Of course, Sharpay has already vowed to be back next year, and you can bet that when that girl puts her mind to something, she never quits!

All About Sharpay Evans

Best Friends: Ryan Evans, Ms Darbus

Quote: "I've already picked out the colours for my dressing room."

Activities: Drama Club (co-president), Autumn Play, Holiday Talent Show, Winter Musical, Spring Musical

Never seen without: a mirror

Where will you be in ten years?

"Accepting my third Tony award. Don't worry. I will thank the little people."

Sharpay congratulates Gabriella on winning the lead in the Winter Musical.

Sharpay does a little digging (for information) in chemistry class.

When Sharpay found out that Gabriella and Troy were called back for second auditions, she had a little trouble maintaining her cool.

Sharpay and Ryan hear something they don't like.

CHAD DANFORTH

Anyone who has met Chad knows he's all about basketball. He would do anything for the team, including trying to convince Troy Bolton not to audition for the Winter Musical. Chad may have crazy hair, funky T-shirts and three watches (anyone know what *that's* about?), but at heart he is a man of tradition. He knows more about the history of the Wildcats basketball team than anyone else in school and once things started to get a little wacky with everyone confessing their hidden talents, he did *not* relish the change.

Chad wanted Troy to stay focused on the championship basketball game so that the Wildcats could bring home the trophy. Can't blame him for that, of course, but he almost robbed us all of watching Troy star in *Twinkle Towne*. Fortunately, he realized he was wrong just in time and, instead of sabotaging Troy, ended up helping him get to his callback. We love a guy who can admit when he's made a mistake. Of course, it was no coincidence that Chad had just started to notice the charms of a certain brainiac, Taylor McKessie. Before Troy and Gabriella shook things up, Chad never would have noticed Taylor, but now, well, he's *definitely* taken an interest.

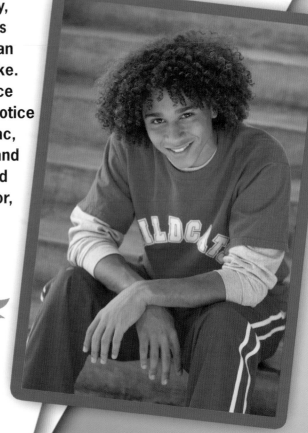

All About Chad Danforth

Best Friends: Troy Bolton, Zeke Baylor, Jason Cross
Quote: "Get your head in the game!"
Sports: Varsity Basketball
Never seen without: his basketball
Where will you be in ten years?
"Leading my team to the NBA championship."

If there's one thing we know Chad is good at, it's firing up the basketball team.

Chad and Troy chill out during tutor group.

Chad gets caught talking in class.

Chad chills with Jason and Zeke.

RYAN EVANS

It's hard to imagine Ryan without his sister, Sharpay. The two of them share everything, from a love of the theatre, to a wealth of talent, to the co-presidency of the Drama Club. Sometimes we think those two must have been born with microphones in their hands! Like Sharpay, Ryan has won the lead in every Drama Club production he's auditioned for (except this year's Winter Musical, of course). He's got a killer voice, some stellar moves and, just like his sister, he's not afraid to go all-out onstage. When it comes to fashion, however, Ryan really has a style all of his own. What other guy at East High owns more hats than he does socks?

When it comes to scheming, Sharpay is the brains of the Evans operation, but that doesn't mean Ryan isn't there to help in any way he can. He helped Sharpay figure out that Troy and Gabriella were interested in trying out for the musical and helped in her attempt to sabotage their auditions. Ryan was just as crushed as Sharpay was when their plan failed, but you can bet he's going to bounce back in a big way. With talent like his, how can he not?

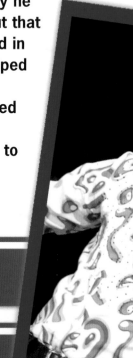

All About Ryan Evans

Best Friends: Sharpay Evans, Ms Darbus

Quote: "Everybody loves a good jazz square."

Activities: Drama Club (co-president), Autumn Play,
Holiday Talent Show, Winter Musical, Spring Musical

Never seen without: a wild hat

Where will you be in ten years?
"Starring on Broadway. Unless Sharpay needs me to back her up.
Then I'll be a backup singer on Broadway."

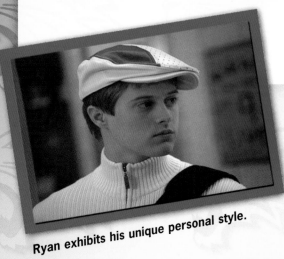

Ryan exhibits his unique personal style.

There's no holding back when Ryan has a microphone in his hands!

Ryan and Sharpay prepare for one of their all-important auditions.

Ryan is moved by one of the auditions for *Twinkle Towne*.

TAYLOR McKESSIE

Taylor McKessie is the smartest girl in school. She maintains a straight-A average while also participating in several academic clubs, including the Scholastic Decathlon team. It had always been Taylor's dream to get the East High team past the first round of the Scholastic Decathlon competition, but as hard as she made her fellow Wildcats study, they just couldn't seem to break out of their rut - until this year. As soon as Taylor found out that new girl Gabriella Montez was something of a brainiac, she recruited her for the team. Together, those two smarties led our squad to their first-ever Scholastic Decathlon victory. Go, girls!

Up until she met her new best friend, Gabriella, Taylor admits she was something of an intelli-snob. She thought all student athletes were on the dim side and even referred to the members of the basketball team as a whole other species. But thanks to Gabriella, Taylor got to know Troy Bolton, Chad Danforth and their friends, and now she can be seen hanging out with all types of people - as long as they don't cut into her study time.

All About Taylor McKessie

Best Friends: Chad Danforth, Gabriella Montez,
other members of the Scholastic Decathlon team
Quote: "I wouldn't consider myself an expert on that particular subspecies."
Activities: Chemistry Club (president), National Honours Society,
Scholastic Decathlon (captain)
Never seen without: her laptop
Where will you be in ten years?
"Receiving my doctorate in biochemistry and accepting my
Nobel Prize for achievement in science."

Taylor and Chad check the time.

If there's a question asked in class, you can
bet Taylor will volunteer to answer it.

Taylor and Gabriella are excited!

Taylor lights up when she finds out she's earned
yet another A!

This year, Kelsi went from music-room hermit to schoolwide star when her compositions were chosen for the Winter Musical. Who knew that shy, perpetually solo Kelsi was hiding an inner artist? Well, we all found out when Troy Bolton and Gabriella Montez performed her incredible tunes onstage. Rumour has it that Kelsi even worked with our star duo to help the onstage amateurs shine for their callbacks. Thanks for that, Kelsi! Without your help, Troy and Gabriella might never have won the leads, and we can't imagine *Twinkle Towne* without them!

All About Kelsi Nielsen

Best Friends: Gabriella Montez, Troy Bolton
Quote: "What key?"
Activities: Winter Musical (composer), Student Orchestra
Never seen without: her sheet music
Where will you be in ten years?
"Hopefully working on Broadway. On some show other than the one Sharpay is starring in."

Kelsi accompanies the hopefuls at Winter Musical auditions.

Kelsi takes Troy and Gabriella's side at callbacks.

Zeke has always been one of the basketball team's highest scorers. Whenever he gets the ball in his hands behind the three-point line, the crowd just knows it'll end in a basket for the Wildcats. But this year, Zeke shocked us all by announcing that he was, in fact, a closet baker. At first, we all thought he was insane. Then we tasted his chocolate-chip cookies. (Heaven!) Let's just say there's more to this particular guy than meets the eye. And it's all in the kitchen! We just can't wait until he perfects that crème brûlée.

All About Zeke Baylor

Best Friends: Troy Bolton, Chad Danforth, Jason Cross
Quote: "I bake. If that helps."
Sports: Varsity Basketball
Activities: Young Bakers of America
Never seen without: something freshly baked
Where will you be in ten years?
"I'll either have my own cooking show or I'll be playing centre for the Phoenix Suns. Or both."

Zeke flashes his pearly whites in class.

Zeke hangs with Chad and Jason before class.

ZEKE BAYLOR

TOP OF THE CLASS!

There's one thing that can always be said about East High: we have a lot of talent at this school! We wanted to show the world exactly how bright our stars shine, so we gave you, the students of East High, a chance to vote in eight major categories. Check out the results of your ballots!

BEST DRESSED: SHARPAY EVANS

Every day our Sharpay turns the halls of East High into her very own runway. She even keeps a change of clothes in her locker, just to keep us all on our toes.

NICEST SMILE: GABRIELLA MONTEZ

What's the first word that comes to mind when you think of Gabriella Montez? Well, aside from "smart" and "talented"? We've got one: supersweet. And she has the smile to go with it!

BEST HAIR: CHAD DANFORTH

Okay, so when you sit behind him in class or in the auditorium, you don't get to see a thing. But doesn't that gorgeous mane of curls make it all worth it?

NICEST EYES: RYAN EVANS

He may not be the brightest bulb in all of East High, but who cares when he's got a pair of baby blue eyes like those?

MOST LIKELY TO SUCCEED: TAYLOR MCKESSIE

This is no shock to anyone. Taylor has been first in our class since we were all bringing lunch boxes to school. We all know she's going to go on to great things!

MOST ATHLETIC: TROY BOLTON

Sometimes, it seems as if Troy can sink every shot he tries to make. He practises hard and loves the game, and his performance on the court truly shows it!

MOST MUSICAL: KELSI NIELSEN

Kelsi may have been hiding behind the scenes for years, but thanks to her creation, *Twinkle Towne*, we now know exactly who she is - and we all appreciate her incredible talent!

CLASS COUPLE: GABRIELLA MONTEZ AND TROY BOLTON

It's hard to believe that these two cuties haven't been together forever. Together, they changed the entire social scene at East High. Now we can't imagine a time when they couldn't be found walking in the halls hand in hand.

MATSUI

PRINCIPAL

Principal Matsui has more school spirit than anyone at East High, and that's saying a lot. Not only does he support our student athletics, but he loves the arts and sciences as well. Okay, so maybe he favours sports a *little* bit - he did choose to attend the basketball championship game rather than the Scholastic Decathlon match or the musical callbacks - but what do you expect from a guy who keeps a mini basketball net in his office? Still, we all know that if there's something we need, whether it's help welcoming a new student or settling a dispute, Principal Matsui will be there. We couldn't ask for a better leader for our school!

All About Principal Matsui

Quote: "We are one school, one student body, one faculty."
Never seen without: a jacket and tie
Where will you be in ten years? "Retired on a beach somewhere."

MS DARBUS

When it comes to drama, Ms Darbus is an expert - and we're not just talking about the theatre. Ms Darbus can make any situation dramatic, whether it's a tutor group lecture about the evils of mobile phones, a debate with Principal Matsui about the importance of her musical productions, or a throw down with Coach Bolton. (Who can forget the day she stormed the boys' locker room just to get in Coach's face? Talk about making an entrance!) As much as we complain about Ms Darbus's strict rules, we can't help loving her for her quirks. And we know that without her love of the theatre and her attention to detail, our plays and musicals wouldn't be such incredible entertainments.

Ms Darbus is caught in the middle of one of her many, many lectures.

Coach gives Jason some pointers at practice.

Coach Bolton is a true East High Wildcat. Not only did he lead the Wildcats basketball team to the championship as a player back in 1981, but he came back to his old school to coach his beloved 'Cats. He's also father to the team's biggest star, Troy Bolton. There are some good b-ball genes in that family! Coach has a bit of a one-track mind when it comes to basketball, however. He's all about practising, focusing and winning. During the season, his players are expected to concentrate on basketball alone, so you can bet that Troy's auditioning for the musical completely threw him. Luckily, he soon got used to the idea that Troy could be fabulous at both. Together, the Bolton men led the Wildcat team to their first championship season in three years and Coach was front and centre on opening night of *Twinkle Towne* to watch his son perform. Now that's what we call Wildcat pride.

Coach Bolton gathers the team, with his whistle and clipboard in hand, of course!

All About Coach Bolton

Quote: "The team is you, and you are the team."
Never seen without: his whistle and clipboard
Where will you be in ten years?
"Watching my son play guard for the L.A. Lakers."

COACH BOLTON

All About Ms Darbus

Quote: "Proximity to the arts is cleansing for the soul."
Never seen without:
a bucket of confiscated mobile phones
Where will you be in ten years?
"Exposing a new generation of students to the magic of the theatre."

Ms Darbus participates in her second-favourite pastime - collecting mobile phones. Her first is, obviously, the theatre.

OUR FAVOURITE PLACES

As dedicated students of East High School, we spend a whole lot of time in these hallowed halls. Whether we're working hard, playing hard, or just chilling with friends, here are some of our favourite places to hang.

The Gym

Our faithful basketball team spends so much time here, the place is starting to smell like them. After-school practices, weekly games, even free-period workouts - you can always find Troy, Chad, Zeke, Jason, or one of the other guys (maybe all of them) out on the court. And we hear that one Gabriella Montez has been hanging out there, too. Hmmm. Wonder what brings a mathlete to the sweatiest room in school . . . ?

The Auditorium

A lot of people hang out in the auditorium by choice, of course Sharpay, Ryan and Kelsi among them. But thanks to Ms Darbus's wacky idea of detention, as well as frequent mobile-phone related punishments - many of us also hang out there because we're forced to. Still, helping out with the sets for the Winter Musical is not the worst way to pass the time in detention. It's kind of fun, actually. Unless, of course, you're Chad.

The Music Room

This is the number one place to go if you're looking to find members of the student orchestra, the marching band, or the jazz ensemble. You can also find Kelsi Nielsen there, pretty much 24/7. Even when she's supposed to be in biology class! (You didn't hear that from us!) This year, Troy Bolton and Gabriella Montez were spotted there during quite a few of their free periods as well, making it one of the most happening places to hang.

ⒺThe Cafeteria

We all love the cafeteria. How could we not?
It's where all the best gossip is heard and all
the greasiest cheese fries are consumed.
(Unless they happen to be all over Sharpay's
outfit.) This year, the cafeteria was the
site of one of the most improbable days in
East High history - the day when everyone
suddenly started confessing all their
innermost dreams and hidden talents.
That's a day none of us will soon forget!

ⒺThe Rooftop Garden

Up until this year, only the members of the
Science Club knew about East High's rooftop
garden. After all, they were the ones who
planted all those luscious flowers and
greenery. But it turns out this is also one of
Troy Bolton's favourite places to catch some
quiet alone time. Or not so alone.

ⒺThe . . . Bathroom?

Well, Sharpay likes to hang there, anyway.
Where else can she find so many mirrors in
one place?

THE WINTER MUSICAL

Ms Darbus and the Drama Club present . . .
TWINKLE TOWNE!

SET CREW

Pop into the auditorium on any given day after school and you'll see dozens of students painting backdrops, hammering sets together and sewing costumes. No, the set crew hasn't doubled its volunteers this year. This is detention! During her preparations for this year's Winter Musical, Ms Darbus found a creative way to get a few extra hands on her crew. Anyone who was given detention by Ms Darbus was forced to work off their time in the auditorium. And she handed out a *lot* of detentions. Check out a few of our favourite memories from the "set crew."

Troy displays his stapling expertise.

Ryan and Sharpay get their hands dirty.

Ms Darbus tells Sharpay and Gabriella to get back to work. She does not appreciate slackers.

Gabriella gives the moon an extra coat of shimmering paint.

Kelsi accompanies Cyndra during her operatic audition.

Troy and Gabriella "audition." Truth is, they don't even know that Ms Darbus is listening!

Ryan and Sharpay strike a pose.

Ms Darbus looks a tad distressed at the quality of talent available for her musical.

FIRST-ROUND AUDITIONS

The auditions for *Twinkle Towne*, this year's Winter Musical, were eventful to say the least. At first, Ms Darbus looked a bit . . . concerned. Apparently, the hopefuls weren't quite up to her exacting standards. After an hour of auditions, she finally put Sharpay and Ryan Evans onstage to show everyone how it's done. And, boy, did they ever show 'em! It looked like Sharpay and Ryan had the leads locked up, as always, until Gabriella Montez and Troy Bolton showed up. At first, Ms Darbus wasn't going to let them try out because they were late, but they sang for fun anyway, and Ms Darbus couldn't ignore their talent. Gabriella and Troy were on their way to a callback!

CALLBACKS

Callbacks for *Twinkle Towne* were a little, shall we say, nutty? Originally, the callbacks were scheduled for a Thursday afternoon. Then Sharpay and Ryan convinced Ms Darbus to move them to Friday - the very same day as the basketball championship game *and* the Scholastic Decathlon match. At first, it looked as if Troy Bolton and Gabriella Montez weren't going to be able to make it to their auditions. Troy started the game with the team in the gym and Gabriella was at the Decathlon in her lab coat with *her* team. Meanwhile, Sharpay and Ryan hit the stage, going all out on a crazy salsa number they had prepared especially for the callback. It looked as if, once again, Sharpay and Ryan were going to be headlining the Winter Musical.

Troy finds out that callbacks have been rescheduled.

Sharpay and Ryan prepare before taking the stage.

Troy and Gabriella beg Ms Darbus for a chance to audition, even though they are late.

Sharpay makes her argument to keep Gabriella and Troy from auditioning.

The auditorium fills up before Gabriella and Troy's callback.

But then, thanks to some bizarre electrical malfunctions in the gym and the lab, Troy and Gabriella were able to make the callbacks. After a bit of a rocky start, the pair got their song on and brought the house down. Oh, did we mention that the auditorium was filled with the Decathlon spectators *and* everyone who had vacated the gym? Troy and Gabriella's audition was more like a sold-out concert, and by the end it was clear who the fans' favourites were. Ms Darbus awarded the leads to Troy and Gabriella, and Sharpay and Ryan were forced to take supporting roles. That's showbiz!

SCHOLASTIC DECATHLON

This year, Scholastic Decathlon captain Taylor McKessie vowed that her team would get past the preliminary round for the first time ever. She assembled a stellar team, but she needed that one well-rounded student who would give them the edge on West High School. So when she found out that transfer student Gabriella Montez was something of an Einstein-ette, Taylor immediately invited her to join the team. Gabriella was resistant at first, wanting to get settled at East High before taking on any extracurricular activities, but Taylor didn't give up and eventually Gabriella joined the team. Now Taylor had her superstar and the group got right to work preparing for the big competition against our rival, West High. Day in and day out, Taylor, Gabriella and their teammates could be found in the lab or one of the classrooms, going over everything from chemistry to calculus to the history of ancient Egypt. These kids are dedicated!

A judge checks Gabriella's work.

The notorious stinky beaker starts to cause trouble.

Taylor asks Gabriella to join the team.

The teams get ready to start the Decathlon.

The Scholastic Decathlon team takes notes from Gabriella.

The day of the Decathlon finally arrived. Gabriella won the first round, deciphering the problem way before her rival had a chance to finish. But then things got a little smelly when a beaker overheated and stank up the room. There was a bit of an intermission, if you will, during which Gabriella rocked her callback for *Twinkle Towne*. Soon after, everyone was back in the lab and East High came through with the victory. Nice work, Captain McKessie! You and your team finally reversed the curse!

VARSITY BASKETBALL

From the very beginning of the season, our Wildcats basketball team was focused on one goal: winning the district championship. Coach Bolton worked the team as hard as he could, whenever he could: after school, during free periods, even on select weekends. Not that the guys minded. Dedicated to East High glory, these 'ballers lived and breathed basketball. If you visited the gym at any moment of any day, you'd find at least one of the guys there practising their jump shots, especially Captain Troy Bolton.

Troy takes the ball upcourt.

Coach is excited by the team's progress.

Chad shows off his skills.

Troy gets ambushed by the team.

Troy tries to get his head back in the game with an extra practice at home.

GET'CHA HEAD IN THE GAME!

But somewhere along the line, things started to change - at least for Troy. He missed a practice here, a workout there, and Coach Bolton and the rest of the team started to question his dedication. Troy insisted that he still had his head in the game, but when the team found out that he was planning to audition for the musical, they really lost it. They even cornered Troy in the locker room and gave him a lecture to remind him of what it means to be a true East High Wildcat. Moved by his teammates' passion, Troy promised he wouldn't let the team down.

The Wildcats cheerleaders perform their pre-game routine.

Principal Matsui makes the announcement to vacate the gym.

THE BIG CHAMPIONSHIP GAME:
East High vs. West High!

The day of the championship game, the East High gymnasium was packed with fans and alive with intensity. The Wildcats were totally pumped and Troy was clearly keeping to his promise. He didn't miss a single shot in the first quarter, hitting everything from layups to three-pointers to foul shots. It looked like the Wildcats were unstoppable, but then . . . something stopped them.

An electrical malfunction caused the scoreboard to flash and all the lights in the gym started going on and off. Principal Matsui was forced to evacuate the gym until the problem could be fixed. The Wildcats' victory was put on hold, but the timing was just right for Troy to make it to the *Twinkle Towne* callback with Gabriella!

VICTORY!

After the problem was fixed and everyone was allowed to return to the gym, Troy and the boys got out there and played like nothing had happened. In fact, Troy even seemed a bit more energized than he was in the first half. (Hmmmm . . . could that be because he'd spent the break singing with Gabriella and winning the lead in the musical?) It didn't take long for the Wildcats to put West High away for good. Troy and his teammates had brought the championship trophy home for the first time in three years! Let the celebration begin!

. . . and makes it! The Wildcats win the game!

As the final seconds tick down, Troy takes his shot. . . .

East High wins the tip-off and gets the ball!

RUMOUR HAS IT!

What would a school year be without juicy gossip? Here are some of the biggest stories of the year.

We hear . . .

Gabriella and Troy actually met during winter break, before Gabriella ever set foot in East High. Were they plotting to take over the musical from Sharpay and Ryan even then?

We hear . . .

Chad's mum keeps a picture of Broadway star Michael Crawford in their refrigerator. Parents are weird.

We hear . . .

Taylor McKessie was responsible for the blackout during the championship game. Well, if anyone has the brains to pull off something like that, it's her!

We hear . . .

Troy sings in the shower. What we wouldn't give to hear a recording of that!

We hear . . .

Zeke is flirting with Sharpay. He invited her to watch one of his games but didn't win her attention until she tasted his chocolate-chip cookies.

We hear . . .

Principal Matsui is a basketball fanatic. He even has a ball and a mini backboard in his office.

 ## *We hear . . .*

Sharpay spends hours a week practising that autograph of hers.
No kidding - it's a work of art.

 ## *We hear . . .*

Chad has been behind on his homework since preschool. If he spent half as much time on his studies as he does playing basketball, this would not be a problem.

 ## *We hear . . .*

Ryan Evans is a huge Ashton Kutcher fan. Who could blame him?

 ## *We hear . . .*

Troy was so scared to audition for the musical, he hid behind a janitor's cart.

 ## *We hear . . .*

Ms Darbus uses all the mobile phones she grabs to call her friends in London's theatre district. (Just kidding!)

 ## *We hear . . .*

Taylor and Gabriella both bite their nails. Who needs healthy nail beds when you've got straight As?

Dear Troy,

We're so proud of you and all that you've accomplished this year, both on the court and on the stage! We can't wait to see what you do next!

Love,
Mum and Dad

Dear Coach Bolton,

Thanks for everything. We couldn't have made it to the championship game without you! GO WILDCATS!

From,
The Varsity
Basketball Team

Dear Taylor,

Straight As and the Scholastic Decathlon victory? As always, you exceed our expectations. We love you!

Love,
Mother and Father

Dear Gabriella,

Remember how nervous you were about starting at East High? And look at all you've achieved. I couldn't be more proud of your courage, intelligence and talent.

Love,
Mum

Dear Zeke,

You bake one mean crème brûlée.

Sincerely,
Your friends at the
Bakers Institute
of America

Dear Chad,

Whoo-hoo!
Go Wildcats!
You did it, kid!

Love,
Mum and Dad

Dear Kelsi,

Next stop, Broadway!
Your musical was
beautiful and inspired.
We love you!

Love,
Mum and Dad

Dear Sharpay and Ryan,

You will always be the biggest stars in the universe to us!

Love,
Your Proud Parents

To the Scholastic Decathlon Team,

We did it! Congrats to the first East High team to win it all!

Love,
Taylor

To the students and faculty of East High,

I WILL be back! You can count on that.

Kisses!
Sharpay

Dear Troy,

Remember New Year's Eve? That wasn't just the start of something new. It was the start of everything. Thanks for transporting me back to kindergarten.

xo
Gabriella

Dear Gabriella,

The moment I realized you had transferred to East High was the best moment of the year. Thanks for helping me see I could be more than just "the basketball guy."

;)
Troy

Dear Ms Darbus,

Thanks for your incredible direction and vision and for introducing us to the joys of the theatre!

Love,
The Cast and Crew of Twinkle Towne

Dear Coach Bolton,

Perhaps there's room here at East High for both of us after all. Congratulations on your big win.

Best,
Ms Darbus

We're All in This Together

So there you have it, our year at East High in a nutshell. It was a crazy year: new friends were made, boundaries were crossed and walls were busted down. There may have been some plotting and scheming along the way, but everything turned out okay. Actually, everything turned out perfectly! Because in the end, we realized that no matter who won or lost, we were all in it together. And that's exactly the way we like it!
Until next year . . .

Go Wildcats!

Sincerely,
The East High School Yearbook Staff